Always VVe Begin Again

The Benedictine Way of Living

Revised Edition

John McQuiston II

Morehouse Publishing
NEW YORK · HARRISBURG · DENVER

Morehouse Publishing, 4775 Linglestown Road, Harrisburg, PA 17112

Morehouse Publishing, 445 Fifth Avenue, New York, NY 10016

Morehouse Publishing is an imprint of Church Publishing Incorporated.
www.churchpublishing.org

Library of Congress Cataloging-in-Publication data:

McQuiston, John.
  Always we begin again : the Benedictine way of living / John McQuiston II.
      p. cm.
  This book is based on The Rule of St. Benedict written by St. Benedict in
the sixth century in Italy.
  Includes bibliographical references.
  ISBN 0-8192-1648-8 (pbk.)
  ISBN-13 978-0-8192-1648-8 (pbk.)
  ISBN-13 978-0-8192-2453-8 (E-book)
  1. Benedict, Saint, Abbot of Monte Cassino. Regula.   2. Monasticism
and religious orders—Rules.   3. Benedictines—Rules.   4. Spiritual
life—Christianity. Benedict, Saint, Abbot of Monte Cassino. Regula.
English. II. Title.
BX3004.A2M37 1996
255'.106—dc20   95-52770
                                                                      CIP

Printed in the United States of America

Praise for

Always We Begin Again

"*John McQuiston II takes the Benedictine rule and adapts it to the circumstances of contemporary life. McQuiston provides one of the most practical tools available for the devout layperson who seeks a daily Christian praxis within the strictures of a successful business or professional life.*"

— Publishers Weekly

"*Here's a book that can become a companion in life, encouraging new insight each time it is read. This is a book I'm going to buy in handfuls and give to all my friends.*

"*This book presents insight that is both ancient and radical. Your mind (and your friends) may call it crazy but your heart and soul will immediately leap to embrace the truth in it.*

"*Within each person is a monastic dimension, usually covered over by anxiety and other burdens. This book calls forth (that) dimension... nurtures it and inspires possibility.*

"*In a world burdened with too many dead ends, this book says to modern people who live in the real world: there is hope.*"

— The Rev. Randall C.K. Day, Executive Director,
The Cathedral Trust in America

CONTENTS

Preface to the Revised Edition: Monks, Brains and Happiness

Almost everything monks and nuns do is good for them. EEG and MRI observations of the brains of Tibetan monks while they are engaged in their traditional loving kindness meditation reveal pronounced increases in electrical activity and blood flow in the left pre-frontal cortex. This is a part of the brain associated with states of happiness and well being. Similar studies of Carmelite nuns engaged in Centering Prayer demonstrate comparable results. Both practices involve maintaining a meditative state in which the mind is focused on thoughts of love.

The Rule of Saint Benedict prescribes these daily activities: attending services of prayer and chant; observing the "lesser silence" during the day, and the "greater silence" at night; engaging in *lectio divina*, the slow, purposeful study of a sacred text, usually the Bible; and performing acts of altruism, hospitality, compassion, and loving kindness to one another and to those in need. The Rule also decrees that all duties be performed cheerfully.

In addition to the reports of the positive effect on the brain of states of meditation or prayer focused on thoughts of love, other studies reveal the following about common monastic practices:

Maintaining loving thoughts increases serotonin levels. Serotonin is a natural chemical that tends to reduce anxiety and increase calmness.

Multinational surveys reveal that in every culture the people who report being the most satisfied with life are its more altruistic members.

Volunteers who were assigned to spend money on others experienced greater happiness than those assigned to spend money on themselves.

Simply being in silence reduces stress and blood pressure.

Persons who meditated daily for two or more months were less depressed, anxious, and angry than before.

Choral singing and chant raise serotonin levels.

Being cheerful and smiling release endorphins and serotonin into the bloodstream, and reduce blood pressure. Endorphins are natural chemicals, which have a morphine-like effect.

Persons engaged in regular meditation produce less of the stress hormone cortisol. They have reduced risk of heart attack and stroke.

Regular periods of focused concentration, such as during meditation and *lectio divina*, fight dementia. In fact, meditation is prescribed as a treatment for dementia. Contrary to previous assumptions, it is now known that new growth can be accomplished even in older brains.

The more human beings practice any behavior, including the maintenance of certain thought patterns, the more the brain responds by embedding that behavior in its dendrites. Dendrites are branches of nerve fibers through which the brain's neurons communicate with each other. Repetition of behavior, whether one's tennis serve or certain thoughts, causes the connections related to that behavior to strengthen.

In a word, common monastic practices produce well being. This should not surprise us. Jesus told us two thousand years before modern medical science that the kingdom of God is an inner state. When he was confronted by the Pharisees, who demanded: "When shall the kingdom of God come?," Jesus answered "The kingdom of God is not found through observation, neither is it found by looking here or looking there, for the kingdom of God is within you" (Luke 17:20-22).

In the twenty years since I was introduced to the Rule of Saint Benedict, I have become convinced that the unstated, central, principle of the Rule is that Christianity was intended to be, and should be, a particular way of "being in the world." It should be a way of life, a way followed by being a person of loving kindness, a compassionate person, a person in caring relationship with one's neighbor. It should never be mere belief.

I say "mere belief" intentionally. Beliefs are made of words, and words are limited, flawed, human expressions. To borrow an image from the Buddhist tradition, words are only fingers pointing, not the object to which they point. It is not too strong to say that the assertion by any group that it possesses the ultimate statement of "correct" belief is an idolatrous claim to know the mind of God. Such claims cause division, conflict, discrimination, and worse.

Love, and in that word I include kindness, altruism, compassion, and empathy, should be paramount to statements of faith, however revered. "Though I have all faith so to move mountains and have not love, I am nothing" (1 Corinthians 13:2).

Saint Benedict's Rule is a way of being in the world. Jesus' life exemplified a way of being in the world. "I am the way, the truth and the light" (John 14:6). We usually think of truth as a set of propositions, but the Bible speaks of a truth that is lived. "Let us love, not in word or speech, but in truth and in action" (1 John 3:18). "The word became flesh and dwelt among us" (John 1:14).

Jesus taught the preeminence of compassionate living over correct belief. He told the story of the Priest and Levite who, no doubt, professed all the correct religious beliefs. However, they walked past the wounded man on the other side of the road, in contrast to the Samaritan, a heretic, who stopped to take care of him (Luke 10:30-37).

The ancient teaching of the paramount importance of maintaining an attitude of love was confirmed in Jesus' reply to the question of the greatest commandment:

Then one of them, a lawyer, asked him a question, tempting him: "Master, which is the greatest commandment in the law?" Jesus replied, "You shall love the Lord your God with all your heart, and with all your soul, and with all your mind. This is the first and great commandment. And the second is like unto it, 'You shall love your neighbor as yourself.' On these two commandments hang all the law and the prophets" (Matthew 22:35–40).

In this passage Jesus cited Jewish scriptures that predated him by centuries: Deuteronomy 6:4-5, known as the Shema, said by Jews for centuries and said today: "Hear, O Israel: The Lord our God is one Lord; and you shall love the Lord your God with all your heart, and with all your soul, and with all your might"; and Leviticus 19:18: "You shall not take vengeance, nor bear any grudge against the children of your people, but you shall love your neighbor as yourself."

I am convinced no one comes to the kingdom of God that is within each of us except by living the way of love. All who live in love, and only those who live in love, enter that kingdom, and they do so regardless of differences in the words they use to express beliefs. Love is not a belief. It is attitude and action.

The two themes of this preface reinforce one another. Medical studies report the positive physiological effects of meditating on, and living in, loving kindness, corroborating the wisdom of the Bible and the Rule. We are, in the words of Psalm 139, "wonderfully made" because we are made to find "the kingdom of God within" through the way of love.

With these thoughts in mind I have revised the text to make a change in emphasis. The original edition emphasized thankfulness, and this revision emphasizes loving kindness, which more fully suggests mutuality and community. It continues to be my hope, as it was in connection with the initial text, to put the wisdom of the Rule to work in my life, and when I fail (as I do consistently) to begin again.

John McQuiston II
Advent 2010

Foreword to the Revised Edition

What exactly defines a book as a "classic" has never been entirely clear to me, even after my many years of dealing both with books and with the various descriptors of their relative status. Lacking a clear definition, I have become, over those same years, more and more averse to attaching the label of "classic" to any book, lest I be found unable to defend so substantial an assessment. That having been said, I now am making bold to say that *Always We Begin Again* is indeed a classic, if ever any book were.

It has been a bit over fifteen years now since the first edition of *Always* was published; and I have long since lost count of the number of folk who, over those fifteen plus years, have praised the book to me, or cited it in overheard conversations with others, or sometimes just quietly confessed to its benefit and blessing in their lives. Other printings have happened, of course. A few years ago, a gift edition was even

issued. It was fatter than the original, because
by custom gift editions always are fatter than
their originals; but no substantive changes or
additions have been made until now. Now,
there are some changes, and the "Revised" in
"Revised Edition" is fairly stated.

John McQuiston's intention, from the very
first, had been, and continues to be, that of
transporting the spirit and wisdom of *The Rule
of St. Benedict* out of its original, sixth-century
language and external circumstances into the
rhetoric and circumstances of our own time
and place. In doing this initially, McQuiston
emphasized in particular the relationship
between Benedict's instruction in *The Rule* and
the role of thankfulness in the fully matured
(or maturing) soul. Now, as he comes again
to address these issues, he lifts up for us the
even more central place of loving kindness as
lynchpin.

"I am convinced," he writes in his Preface to
this Revised Edition, "that no one comes to the
Kingdom of God that is within each of us except
by living the way of love. All who live in love, and
only those who live in love, enter that kingdom.
And they do so regardless of differences in the

words they use to express beliefs. Love is not a belief. It is attitude and action."

McQuiston's assertion is far more sinewy than one might, at first blush, think, however. Arguing gracefully but convincingly like the successful lawyer he is, John McQuiston makes his case — and Benedict's — for the imperative of a basic and God-tuned rhythm in one's daily life. Only that set rhythm of prayer and rest and refreshment, hospitality and quiet, he argues, effectually tutors and steels the human life, thereby opening it to the state of loving kindness and its exercise.

By "translating" *The Rule* into the language and exigencies of "those whose lives, like mine, occur primarily outside church and monastery," McQuiston provides us with far more than a mere "classic" of a book, though. He provides us here a kind of illuminated map, if you will, into the intentional life and into a kind of sweet carefulness for every irreplaceable hour of our irreplaceable lives. Living the Kingdom ceases to be some metaphor for the vaguely conceptualized and becomes instead a direction toward which we are both commanded and intended for.

I was recently engaged in one of those purely social conversations in which a man whom I had never met before said to a woman I did not know very well, ". . . but I do, of course, have McQuiston's *Always We Begin Again*, and that makes such a difference."

"Oh," she said, "I must get a copy and read it, then."

. . . to which, and somewhat to my own surprise, I heard myself saying, "Oh, no! It's not a book you 'read.' It's a book you absorb."

I'm not sure that she understood what I was telling her at the time, though I certainly hope that she does by now. In either event, though, I am certain that those of us who engage *Always* here will know very quickly that we are holding in our hands a book that, to use the old phrase, is to be inwardly digested, a book that, as I tried to tell my acquaintance, is to be, not read, but lived.

Phyllis Tickle
Compiler, *The Divine Hours*

About the Rule

The Rule of Saint Benedict is a set of directions for monastic life written by Benedict of Nursia in the sixth century in Italy. Benedict was educated in Rome at a time when pagan Arian tribes had overrun the civilized world. The church was torn by conflict, and civil and religious authorities were corrupt. Repelled by the vices of Rome, Benedict left the city for the solitude of the hills of Subiaco. In that rocky country he lived in a cave for three years. A monk named Romanus was his mentor. While living as a hermit, he developed a reputation as a holy man.

On the summit of a cliff overlooking Anio there was a community of monks whose Abbot had died. They persuaded Benedict to replace him. However, Benedict's ideas about monastic discipline apparently did not suit them. Legend has it that they attempted to poison his wine, but he became aware of the poison before drinking, made the sign of the cross over the jug, broke it, and asked God to forgive them. He then returned to Subiaco and began his life's work. Benedict established monasteries in which the monks were to be committed to a set of ideals, and were to follow a rhythmic daily pattern of work, study, community, and prayer. He founded twelve monasteries at Subiaco, near Rome, and the abbey at Monte Cassino.

The Rule of Benedict revitalized the Western monastic movement. Benedictine monks established monasteries throughout Europe. Benedictines carried Christianity into Western Europe and the British Isles. Most of the great European cathedrals, and their related universities, came from Benedictine roots. When the Roman Empire collapsed, the monasteries were among the few institutions that kept society functioning.

The monastic movement, empowered by Benedict's Rule, reached its peak influence in the Middle Ages. Between its origin and the Reformation, fifty popes, thirty emperors, and ninety-seven kings and queens were, or claimed to be, Benedictines. Yet as the Benedictine movement became a secular and political power, it departed from its origins and values, and declined.

Nevertheless, the Rule of Saint Benedict is more than a chapter in the history of Western civilization. At its core is a series of remarkable insights into the art of living. Since the sixth century many thousands of sincere people, from varied backgrounds and from every part of the globe, have discovered the Rule to be a reliable guide to a profoundly satisfying way of life.

The Rule contains a singular collection of bearings. It is pragmatic and concrete — requiring tangible daily action and a continuing commitment to leading a balanced life. At the same time it is deeply idealistic — requiring a persistent effort to transcend self-centered existence.

Benedict knew that we are creatures of habit, and his Rule recognizes our need to develop and maintain a basic rhythm for life. He also was aware that we are communal creatures, and that we must seek out companions who will support us in our long-term efforts. From these and many other insights he created a manual for living that has inspired and supported countless thousands for more than 1,400 years.

Unfortunately the Rule of Saint Benedict has been largely lost to our time. While active Benedictine abbeys and monasteries still function throughout the world, their number and influence are small. The Rule itself is written in a context and language that means little to our secular culture. Very few of us share the same world view or religious beliefs as Saint Benedict. Almost none of us want to, or could, retire to a monastery. Nevertheless, at the heart of the Rule is a core of truth about the human condition. It contains a series of brilliant insights concerning how one may make ordinary life into something deeply fulfilling.

There is increasing recognition in medical science that the human mind contributes to, and in some sense creates, the universe in which it lives. Discoveries in physics confirm that the act of observation is inextricably linked to, and changes, the "reality" observed. This knowledge corroborates the critical role of our own attitudes and perspectives in shaping the world in which we live. The Rule of Saint Benedict is consistent with these discoveries. It is grounded in the realization that the ways we relate to life, our daily actions, thoughts, and feelings, reshape our universe.

The Rule teaches that if we take control of our lives, if we are intentional and careful in how we spend the hours of each irreplaceable day, if we discipline ourselves to live in a balanced and thankful way, we will create from our experiences, whatever they may be, the best possible life. Surely this knowledge is as invaluable now as it was in the sixth century.

My Introduction
to the Rule

My acquaintance with the Rule of Saint Benedict began when unrelated events repeatedly placed it in my path. I am a middle-aged lawyer with a busy commercial practice. Like many others my age I have been a lifelong church member, but I have never been comfortable with the idea that any one religion has a corner on truth. For the most part, I have not found church services to have been particularly meaningful, especially when compared with the influence of other institutions and experiences. Prior to my exposure to the Rule, no religious exercise or practice had ever been a part of my everyday life.

Some years ago my father died. During the weekend of his funeral I met an Episcopal priest who had been my father's close friend and golfing companion. He was about my age, and we quickly became friends. I shared with him my disappointment that the church had played a much greater role in my father's life than in my own. In one of several conversations we had during that weekend he recommended a book to me. He could not remember the exact title, but he recalled the subject and the author's name — Esther de Waal. Later I learned that the title was *Living With Contradiction: Reflections on the Rule of St. Benedict.*

The following summer, through an opportunity offered to my wife, our family spent a week living in a dormitory on the grounds of Canterbury Cathedral. Canterbury's origins are Benedictine, and a Benedictine monastery still is functioning near the Cathedral. We learned that Esther de Waal was the wife of the former Dean of Canterbury Cathedral, and we met people who knew her well. While there, we joined a group of friends of Canterbury Cathedral called "The Canterbury Cathedral Trust in America." The Trust had been, and continues to be, experimenting with ways to bring the Benedictine experience to interested people.

After we returned home another priest and friend suggested that I take a few minutes each morning to read the service of Morning Prayer from the Book of Common Prayer.

Establishing the discipline of taking a few minutes each morning to read something uplifting and to think or meditate, began to make a subtle change during the rest of my day. Reading from the Rule of Saint Benedict became a part of that morning time.

Over time I "translated" the Rule and the service of Morning Prayer into my own words. Because the more traditional language and images used by the institutional church and by Saint Benedict had lost much of their ability to communicate to me, my purpose in restating was to make the core insights of the Rule more accessible. I needed to free the underlying methods and principles of the Rule from their original context and terminology to make them relevant to me. Some of these changes were appropriate because I do not live in a monastery. Others resulted for more subtle reasons. For example, because of my particular viewpoint, it felt more authentic for me to speak of the profound mystery of which we are a part, than to use any established religion's name for the Ultimate.

Most significantly I wanted to stress the critical importance of our pattern of response to life, rather than espousing any particular creed. This approach seemed particularly well suited to the Rule, because Saint Benedict's concern was not merely with words and ideas. His is a system meant to be experienced and practiced.

As I was doing this work with the written Rule, I began to try to establish a pattern for each day's activity that was loosely modeled on Benedict's principles. As I became more intentional and thoughtful concerning the shape of my days, and took time for some parts of Benedict's system, my attitudes and feelings began to change in quiet but important ways.

Two years after our summer visit to Canterbury my wife and I attended a three-day Benedictine retreat in an old Victorian home in Manhattan. The Canterbury Cathedral Trust in America sponsored the retreat. I shared my restatement of the Rule with the participants. Several were distinguished church leaders and one was the Abbot of a Benedictine monastery. They were enthusiastic and encouraging; the Abbot later wrote me a long letter with suggestions.

Always We Begin Again makes no claim to be a precisely accurate statement of the original. It is only a paraphrase that, hopefully, is consistent with the spirit of the Rule. It is intended to make the means of the Rule available for use by those whose lives, like mine, occur primarily outside church and monastery. Although the Rule is a great Christian text, and what is said here may be taken in a Christian way, it is not limited to a Christian interpretation.

The Rule sets out a specific daily schedule incorporating work, study, community, and prayer. The monastic day is "ordered," that is, it is divided by seven worship services. While the daily orders of the Benedictine Rule may not be feasible for us, undergirding those specifics are principles that we can use. For example, we can recognize the need for a basic daily pattern that incorporates time not only for work, but also for friendship, the growth of the mind, and for meditation. We can take control of our workdays and build into them time to serve other values. We can establish the habit of stopping throughout the day to be thankful. By such practices we can raise our spirits, and change our perspectives and our lives, perhaps dramatically.

The Rule of St. Benedict is comprised of 73 admonitions intended to assist the difficult task of accomplishing interior changes. None of us enjoys being told what to do, but hopefully we can accept the teaching of this great spritual master as an aid in our quest for a more abundant life.

The Rule of
Saint Benedict

A Contemporary Interpretation

The First Rule

A ttend to these instructions, Listen with the
heart and the mind; they are provided in
a spirit of goodwill.

These words are addressed to anyone
who is willing to renounce the delusion
that the meaning of life can be learned;
whoever is ready
to take up the greater weapon of fidelity
to a way of living that transcends
understanding.

The first rule is simply this:

live this life
and do whatever is done,
in a spirit of loving kindness.

Abandon attempts to achieve security,
they are futile,

give up the search for wealth,
it is demeaning,

quit the search for salvation,
it is selfish,

and come to comfortable rest
in the certainty that those who
participate in this life
with an attitude of compassion
will receive its full promise.

Each Day

At the beginning of each day,
after we open our eyes
to receive the light
of that day,

As we listen to the voices
and sounds
that surround us,

We must resolve to treat each hour
as the rarest of gifts,
and be grateful
for the consciousness
that allows us to experience it,
recalling in thanks
that our awareness is a present
from we know not where,
or how, or why.

When we rise from sleep let us rise for the joy
of the true Work that we will be about
this day,
and considerately cheer one another on.

Life will always provide matters for concern.
Yet each day brings with it reasons for
joy.

Each day carries the potential
to bring the experience of heaven;
have the courage to expect good from it.

Be gentle with this life,
and use the light of life
to live fully in your time.

Paramount Goals

What is wanted is not that we should
find ultimate truth,
nor that we should become secure,
nor that we should have ease,
nor that we should be without hurt,
but that we should love.

There is no fear in love.
Therefore we should not fear life,
nor anything in life,
we should not fear death,
nor anything in death,
we should live our lives
in love with life.

It is for us
to train our hearts
to live in grace,
to sacrifice our self-centered desires,
to find peace without want
without seeking it for ourselves,

and when we fail,
to begin again each day.

If we adopt an outlook of confidence and trust and perfect our experience by care for others, if we live in the certainty that we are heirs in the providence of the outermost mystery, we will begin to change into the persons that we have the potential to be.

Good Works

If you want to live
the life that only you can live,
do good for others,
and when you have done good,
you will have life abundantly.

A life without good works
is a shadow life.
A life centered on itself
is an empty life.

Seek to do good for others,
and you will find fulfillment.
Forget yourself
and you will discover what you are
seeking.

And if we do good works,
we should not do them in the hope of reward,
nor in the desire for betterment,
nor can we be proud or self-righteous
on account of our good works.

We must credit the good we do
to the hidden foundation of good,
and be grateful to serve as its medium.

Each good action we perform is like a
blow from a sculptor's chisel, cutting away
the dross, and shaping the ideal form hidden
within the stone. Each step we take away from
dependence on material possessions is like a
day of training for an athlete, strengthening
ourselves into the fit and healthy persons we
were designed to be. It is the small daily brush
strokes that create the painting, no matter how
large the canvas.

Teaching and Learning

What is taught by example
is more significant than
what is taught by words.

The greatest lesson,
   the way to live, can never be learned by
   rote, but is found only by the practice of
   one's own authentic compassion.

Those who seek to find their genuine course
   need to submit to the direction of wise
   leaders.

And as we each have duties to perform in
   society,
   acceptance of the authority of others is
   also necessary
   for the tasks of the community to be
   accomplished.

One who seeks to teach should strive to
remember what a perilous and serious task it is

to attempt to instruct others. Each of us learns in disparate ways, and finds distinctive paths.

For each person the goal is distinctive in its aspects. For we, as finite creatures, can perceive only what we are capable of perceiving. Therefore each person must be dealt with in accordance with his or her unique disposition and capacities.

Leadership

A fit leader must attune to the variations in people.
A gentle person may be led by persuasion, while the rebellious by more exacting means.

The true leader should never value things above the value of maintaining an attitude of care and compassion.

Those who chose to follow bear the responsibility for their choice of leaders.

When any significant action is to take place, or any important decision is to be made, counsel should be taken in all cases where it is possible to do so. Our actions always have consequences, and the people affected by them should participate in decisions that touch their lives.

We each see the world from divergent viewpoints, and we are equal participants in the cosmic game. For these reasons it is both efficient and right that consultation occur in all matters of substance.

Those who are consulted should give their insights without argument, and should accept the ultimate decision with good grace when it diverges from their point of view.

Once the advice of those involved has been obtained, the person whose responsibility it is to choose a course of action should take counsel alone, and then act as is best in the circumstances. Frequently, all that can be done is to choose from several less-than-perfect alternatives. In those cases we must accept the limitations imposed on us as the natural result of things as they are, and avoid the paralysis that comes from wishing for different circumstances.

In all things be governed by the sense, not the letter, of right principles.

Right Relationship

We all have our own perception of, and relationship to, some God. We may not use the name "God." We may think in terms of Reality, Nature, The First Cause, The Behavior of the World, The Other, The All, The Ground of Being, The Force of Evolution, The Life Spirit, or Things As They Really Are. Each of us creates an image of the supreme mystery that feeds us, and we are always in a relationship with it.

The nature of our concept of what controls life, and the character of our relationship to it, changes according to our perceptions and attitudes. Our relationship can be one of fear or of love, of malaise or of enthusiasm. It can be anything we make it. We must train ourselves. We must learn to turn our thoughts and feelings to vehicles for loving kindness.

Experience is the raw material from which we create our attitude toward, our engagement with, our vision of, our God. We are responsible for our vision, our beliefs. We can make our experience heaven or hell.

These are the opportunities for right relation-ship:
To form a loving image of our God, and
To love our true God, with all our hearts, with all our minds, and with all our strength, and
To love our neighbors as much as we love ourselves.

If we follow the spirit of these charges we will not need any others. But because we are merely human, we should remind ourselves,

to relieve the unhappy,
to visit the sick,
to clothe the destitute,
to shelter the oppressed,

not to take ourselves too seriously,
not to want more than we need,
not to love possessions,
not to carry resentment,

to support the troubled,
to encourage good humor,
to forgive our enemies,
to show mercy to the weak,

   not to want praise,
   not to be proud,
   not to be slothful,
   not to offer unwanted advice,

to pray frequently,
to distrust one's own will,
to speak the truth to ourselves and others,
and to prefer nothing to the habit of affinity.

   These are the tools.

   The workshop in which these tools are
employed is the community of relationships.

Self-Forgetfulness

Our ultimate goal is this: to forget
ourselves.
To be satisfied in life
We must transcend the desire for
satisfaction.
We must cast off our own appetites.
We must free ourselves from our own self-
centeredness.
In order to accomplish this,
we must practice obedience.

The obedient servant subordinates his or her
own will to another.
It is in the servant's long-term interest
to do so.

Likewise, if we are to become strong enough
to emancipate ourselves from the tyranny
of our own cravings,
we must train our constitutions
by the continuous exercise of obedience
to other persons and to the dictates of our
circumstances.

We must always be prepared to cast aside our own agendas whenever we have the opportunity to be of service to another. And when we act for another's interests we must do so cheerfully, without thought of recognition or reward. Our greatest compensation will occur when compensation is not sought.

Silence

Remember the great value of silence.
Each day there must be time for silence,
even in our prayers and meditation.
There must be time within which we
neither speak nor listen,
but simply are.

Consider the silence of a living tree;
it neither speaks nor hears.
Out of the uncounted aeons,
inexorable, ever-changing forces
have erected it,
to a purpose beyond our understanding.
It needs no words,
yet its presence
is no less actual than ours.

Consider the value of silence in community.
Our ability to listen is our gift
to those around us.
Too much talk is sign of self-centeredness
and insecurity.

If you hear yourself talking excessively,
take care.

Humility

Cultivate humility.
To be exalted is to be in danger.

Pride is considered a sin because it warps our
existence.
It establishes our lives on a false foundation.

No one can win all the time.
Therefore, a life based on triumphing over others
will always be unfulfilled.

The way to closeness with the sublime
is not to add,
but is to take away more each day
until we have been freed,
even from desire for perfection.

The Twelve Stages of Humility

These are the stages to freedom from self-
    centeredness,
to humility,
the centerpiece of the true life.

The first stage of humility
is to keep the sacred nature of consciousness
and the world in which it exists
always alive within us.

Everything we think,
everything we do,
everything we feel,
is cast in time forever.
Every moment that we live is irreplaceable,
therefore each moment is hallowed.

We must be on guard
against despair, against fear,
against bitterness, against self-seeking,
and have the tenacity and courage
to think optimistically and act kindly,

and to put the needs of others always before
our own.

The second stage of humility
is to distrust our own will.
Our wants are insatiable,
and our will is the product of those wants.
Our pleasure,
our needs,
our wishes —
all are mere self-interest,
and the demands of self-interest
are never ending.

Our desires are the path to disaster.
At every turn there is something more to
acquire,
something to distract our attention,
something to divert the unchangeable
footprints we leave behind.

Day and night we must return to humility,
and use it as a compass to guide us on the
true course.

Therefore the second stage of humility
is not to love our own will,
nor to find pleasure in the satisfaction of our
own desires,
but to carry out the unfathomable purpose of

our being,
to fulfill the design that can only be
discovered
by overcoming our own cravings —
for the function of existence
and of our lives
is not ourselves.

The third stage of humility
is to accept our limitations,
even to death.
To accept that there are events
outside our control
and that have ultimate power over us,
and that our will
will not be done.

The fourth stage of humility is to be patient
and to maintain a quiet mind,
even in the face of inequity, injury, and
contradiction,
preserving the awareness
that we are ever shaped by
experience
and refined by fire,
and accordingly
to be thankful even for injuries.

The fifth stage of humility
is not to conceal our faults,

but to be ruthlessly honest
with ourselves
and about ourselves,
for to lie to ourselves or to others
is to falsify our relationship with true life.

The sixth stage of humility is to be content
with the work we are given to do
and with the circumstances of our lives
however unfair or demeaning,
always bearing in mind
that it is our outlook
that confers value on our experiences,
and that nothing that occurs to us
is intrinsically good or bad.

The seventh stage of humility
is not only to declare ourselves to be humble,
but to believe in our hearts that we are of no
consequence.

For alone we are of no moment —
in the vast reaches and endless memory of
the universe
our most profound idea is the merest fantasy;
our greatest triumphs
and our meanest actions
are as lasting as a footprint in sand.

The eighth stage of humility
is that we take no action except that which is
in accordance with the path established for
us, by word and by example, by those whom
we know to be true guides, both past and
present, always mistrusting our own ideas
and wills.

The ninth stage of humility
is that we refrain from judgment.
It is not for us to live the lives of others,
or to understand the infinite forces at work
at every instant in another's life.
We must restrain not only our criticism
but also our advice,
offering it only when requested,
and then only with sincere misgiving.

The tenth stage of humility
is to have sincere empathy.
We can never believe ourselves superior to
one another,
nor take pleasure in each other's
shortcomings and misfortunes.

The eleventh stage of humility
is to speak gently and briefly.
Participation in community requires

that we speak, and also that we listen.
In speech we must be candid,
in listening we must be accessible.

The twelfth stage of humility
is to maintain not only humble thoughts,
but also a humble demeanor,
whether at work, on the road, at the
market,
in speaking or at rest.

We should continuously reenforce,
through appearance and demeanor, the
mien of humility.

By daily pursuing these intentions,
we will begin to observe these precepts
through habit rather than by discipline,
and in consequence,
after long practice,
we will sometimes accomplish these goals
as our natural manner.

Routine

We are physical creatures, and creatures of routine. We thrive when a specific daily schedule is established.

The day should be divided
so that there is
time for meditation or prayer,
time for meals and relationships,
time for learning,
time for labor,
and time for rest.

Time for labor and time for rest will consume two-thirds of our hours. But eight hours a day remain for study, meals, sharing, and prayer. The wise use of these eight hours is most often neglected.

Bear in mind that the seasons bring changes. Flexibility is required in all things human. Do not be afraid to vary your schedule as long as you are consistent with the spirit of daily balance.

One day a week we should worship with others, more frequently if we have an opportunity. Solitary meditation or prayer, like solitary life, must be balanced with community. We cannot shift the center of our lives away from ourselves if we are too much alone.

Routine is important, but too much of it dulls. On days of special importance, our routine should be varied, but within limits, always maintaining the spirit of the daily reaffirmation of the way. This spirit allows the daily method to be relaxed and amended from time to time, in keeping with both the sense of freedom and of discipline that we seek. We should modify our prayers and meditations with the seasons, so that from season to season there is change, but from year to year there is repetition.

The routine of the day should vary according to the seasons, but a regular pattern should be followed. Self-discipline should be maintained, for without self-discipline, we will never strengthen our inner resources sufficiently. Without self-discipline we will always be lost.

At the end of each day, time should be strictly reserved for meditation or prayer, and silence. It should be the practice to gather together in the evening for a reading, sharing, or prayer according to your nature, followed by silence. The reading should be appropriate for the time before sleep, and be only a few pages in length. The last devotion before sleep should be chosen carefully, and it should be sung or recited if possible. Music speaks to us in a language beyond words, and the life we are seeking to live is one of harmony and rhythm.

Establish a regular pattern for meditation at night, and follow it.
If your sleep is untroubled, accept the rest you are given.
If you are caught up with concern, meditate and pray.
In the night we are most vulnerable to fear.

Give thanks for your trouble, and accept that life includes trouble as well as joy. All is given out of the mystery that called us into being, and of which we are.

One day a week should be a day of rest and study. We must have time to reflect and to renew. All of our growing and healing is not conscious. We must give ourselves time to mend and germinate.

Create a daily pattern and follow it. Maintain your discipline. Accomplish each task you have set before yourself.

Stewardship

The steward to whom management of material possessions is entrusted should be neither avaricious nor parsimonious. He or she should be realistic and measured in decisions, and should view possessions as a trust.

The most critical quality for a manager, whether of property or persons, is humility. The task of a manager confers power, and he or she must be continually on guard against self-importance and vanity. Frequently such a person will need assistance from others. Help should be sought freely, keeping in mind that neither power nor wealth should be hoarded.

From what we have, those things which should be given are to be given freely and without delay, so that no one shall be angered over possessions. At all times let us recall that every thing we use in this life was here before us and will be here after we are gone. This world and everything in it is on loan, entrusted to our care for our time.

The only significance of things is our relationship with them. The idea that we own anything, or that we created and possess those characteristics that make us what we are, must be utterly rooted out. Let no one presume that we are more than passing shadows, created from we know not what, for a purpose we cannot understand. We are merely tenants at sufferance in this life.

Everything we have is on loan. Our homes, businesses, rivers, closest relationships, bodies, and experiences, everything we have is ours in trust, and must be returned at the end of our use of it. As trustees we have the highest and strictest requirements of fiduciary duty: to use nothing for our sole benefit; to manage prudently; and to return that which has been in our care in as good or better condition than it was when given into our custody.

No one should complain because someone else has more. Our needs should be small, and we should not want that which exceeds what we truly need.

Those who need little should be thankful. Those who believe they need more should seek to correct this defect. The only genuinely wealthy are those who are satisfied with what they have.

The daily consumption of material things should be parsimonious. It is a good thing to deprive oneself of certain needs and comforts periodically, to fast and meditate, and to resume normal life with thanks, renewed appreciation, and joy. The material side of existence should be treated reverently as a gift from that incomprehensible source of all things, and valued as the means of daily life for ourselves and others. But we must be ever on guard against making the material an end.

Service

No one is excused from rendering service to others. No one is exempt from performing the mundane tasks of daily life. Rendering service to others is necessary to our own fitness. Exempting someone from commonplace chores invites vanity.

If one has special talents, they should be used for the benefit of others. On no account should one's talents be cause for vanity. If egotism results from the exercise of a gift, the practice of that talent should cease until it no longer results in hubris.

The use of goods and talents primarily for oneself is incompatible with humility. Humility is the key that unlocks the universe. Living life as if the pursuit of goods and recognition is its purpose, destroys it.

Putting ourselves at the center of existence isolates us. We are relational, dependent creatures, and we are not the purpose of the cosmos. The great unknown and transcendent mystery is its own purpose.

We should share in labor and take turns in service. As a task is handed from one to another, approval and thanks should also be passed from one to another, so that good will and blessings are distributed with the work.

We must care for the sick and visit them. We should deal with them patiently, seeking, through our attention to their need, to practice the art of caring. We must recognize that attending the sick can lead us into a fuller dimension of a fruitful life.

Those of us who are sick should consider that our suffering is a part of incomprehensible reality, and that it is our task and opportunity to make the encounter with illness serve an exalted function. Those who lead must ensure that the sick are not neglected.

Meals

Meals should be taken together in a spirit of community and used as an opportunity to share our interior life. The expression of our thoughts and feelings serves many purposes. Frequently when we speak we open ourselves new insight. We do not know what others feel or think unless they share it through words. Language breaks down our separation. Responsibility for communication is to be shared, so that each member of the group shall take an equal turn.

Only wholesome food should be eaten, and only in an amount which is sufficient to satisfy hunger. Gluttony and excess consumption of any kind must not be tolerated in ourselves. With regard to alcoholic drink, abstinence is desirable, moderation is essential.

Meals should be taken at regular times. We share a physical nature with the rest of creation, and eating is an essential activity. Therefore we should make this vital function play its appropriate role in nurturing the design of the life we seek.

Worship

The adoption of an attitude of thankfulness to the sublime mystery that brought us into being and preserves us is at once means and end. Its worth is beyond measure. Therefore our distance from our regular place for meditation, prayer, and being thankful should never prevent our performing that work for our spirits.

Remember that we are always in the presence of the sacred, but that the sacred nature of life is only apparent to those who are open to it. We are a part of the infinite which is in this moment expressing itself through us and in every facet of daily life.

In order that we live as our best selves, we must maintain an attitude of appreciation for this life and for the eternal mercy that provided it. A service of thanks and praise should be established for worship, containing both the familiar and the inspiring.

If we address persons of distinction, we accord them honor and respect. How much more should we accord the Unknown Source of all that exists and of all relationships. Our attitude in prayer and meditation should therefore be pure and humble.

When we are nearby to our usual place of meditation, we should return to that place at the appointed times, for we are sustained by such continuity. We are physical creatures, and concrete reenforcement of habits of meditation, prayer, and gratefulness will assist us in the work.

Similarly, when we are near to our friends and family at mealtimes, we should take our meals in community, renewing and continuing the relationships that make up the fabric of our lives.

We are ceremonial creatures. A special place for worship services should be maintained, and a place reserved for the cultivation of our spirits.

It should be made available between services for individual prayer and meditation. It should always be treated with reverence, and when services are not taking place a deep silence should be preserved.

We must not allow criticism of the failings of organized religion to keep us from worshiping in community. No one can live up to the standards of the great religions. There is no church, synagogue, or temple that does not contain some number of persons who are sincere, worthy of friendship, and from whom we can learn.

Guests

Guests, like all of us, are representatives of the great mystery at work in creation. They should be conferred honor and welcomed accordingly. Whether a guest is leaving or arriving the greatest humility should be shown.

Special attention should be given to the needy guest. Material wants should be attended to in a way that preserves dignity.

The presence of guests should not, however, be allowed to disrupt the routine that has been established. The work of the day must go on while guests are provided with their due.

We are all guests in the world, and all equally present in time.

Community

It is best to live one's life with the support of a community which shares right values. When someone leaves such a community temporarily, let that person be wary. A human being is especially vulnerable when not supported by others.

Let no one attempt to hide faults or to cover up for another. Hypocrisy is the result of such actions, and hypocritical living is false living. We live in groups, and honesty and candor are essential both to the health of the community and the individuals in it.

Each day we must seek a loving and forgiving heart, for without the cultivation of love and forgiveness we will never be at peace. We will live in love only to the extent that we can truly become forgiving and loving persons ourselves.

When a task seems overwhelming, one may ask for help or for a reduction in the size of the responsibility. Nevertheless, when the job remains to be done, one should move forward to perform it, trusting in that which is greater than we can understand.

Conclusion

This rule and similar precepts should be studied and re-read often. We cannot learn new ways of living without effort. We cannot attain our highest potential selves without discipline and training.

It is a supreme transgression against one's nature to lead a life that is unfaithful to one's own best character. Accordingly, once the correct path is chosen, no departure from that course should be tolerated, for one would, in such a case, be committing a great wrong.

We should exercise the greatest patience with our own and with one another's faults, refraining from judgment.

Neither these words, nor any book, can accomplish what is truly necessary in one's life.

Existence cannot be understood,
only experienced.

The Life we are given to live must be loved,
whatever it brings;
the good we are taught must be put into
practice, whatever our circumstances.

Remember humility.
Humility is the inner attitude of indifference
to oneself
and freedom from oneself.
If you are internally disquiet
you may be assured you do not have
humility.

We must prefer nothing
to the art of caring for others.

*Some Forms
of Meditation and Prayer*

A Form of Centering Prayer

Centering Prayer is an effort to quiet the mind and open ourselves to experience the love of God. It traces its roots to the first Christian monks, known as the Desert Fathers. *The Cloud of Unknowing,* written by an anonymous author in the fourteenth century is a part of that tradition. Here is a method of Centering Prayer adapted from that taught by the Christian monks Basil Pennington and Thomas Keating:

Sit comfortably with your eyes closed, relax, and quiet yourself. Let yourself be open to feel the love of God.

Choose a few words that express your intention to be in God's presence and open to His loving action within you, such as: "Christ Be Within Me," "Come Lord Jesus," "Come Holy Spirit."

Let this idea be present in you as a symbol of your sincere intention to be a vehicle of His loving action within you.

Whenever your thoughts drift return to your chosen words.

Ideally you will pass beyond words into a peaceful realm of God's love.

A Form of Loving Kindness Meditation

Buddhists monks are taught a loving-kindness meditation. It is a part of a 3,000- year-old practice known in the Pali language of India as the Metta Bhavana. In the Buddhist form the meditator "sends" loving kindness to others. In the following adaptation, the meditation is a prayer.

Sit quietly. Take a few deep breaths. Start by praying for loving kindness for yourself. Then pray that loving kindness comes to others:

to loved ones;
to friends;
to a mentor or wisdom figure;
to a person for whom you have neutral feelings;

to a person for whom you have negative feelings;
to all people;
to all beings;
to the universe.

You may find it helpful to say silently: "May _____ be happy, may _____ experience love, may _____ experience peace."

A Morning Prayer

Grace to us and peace.
We are given this day,
and awareness of its colors and sounds.
We receive these and other gifts too
numerous to name
and infinitely rare.
For these gifts,
we are thankful

We do not know what this day will bring —
life is the great enigma;
life is the great good;
we expect good from this day.

At all times, and at this time
we participate in the great Mystery.
We acknowledge our contingent nature.
We humble ourselves before that which we
do not understand.

When we consider the vast reaches of the
cosmos,

the incomprehensible forces at work in each
moment,
the numberless stories of each life,
the millions of forgotten ancestors who
preceded us,
the untold acts of kindness which occur each
day,
We humble ourselves.

We keep silence.

Help us to save ourselves by forgetting
ourselves.
In every experience and thought,
bring us into the certain knowledge
that we are children of the infinite.

Assist us to envision life as an opportunity
to share
in the creation
of a caring environment,
to open our mind's eye to the knowledge
that if we give love,
nothing in life
nor in death,
nor things to come,
nor things past,
can separate us
from the state of grace.

Help us this day
to receive grace
and to give it.

We believe that we are
children of the unlimited
and that we are enveloped in an unbounded
network of friendships, affiliations, and
relationships.
They are in time and beyond time.

We believe in the ancient message
that adopting an attitude of love
toward this life and all that it brings
will profoundly alter our lives and
our universe.

In our activities this day
we ask for the power to be
continuously thankful,
in our words and in our hearts;
to give up concern for ourselves
and thus to walk in perfect freedom.

May the vast mystery beyond comprehension
fill us with joy and peace and love
this day and always.

We lift up our hearts.

A Mid-day Prayer

We give thanks for our existence;
  we recognize that
we rely on forces beyond our understanding.

We trust what this life brings:

we trust ourselves,
we trust our friends,
we trust our families,
we trust life,
we trust the universe.

We release our past to the past,
we release our future to the future,
we accept our present.
We let go of our cares and fears.

We abandon our illusions of control.
We acknowledge our complete dependence
on providence.

We relinquish our apprehension.
We rely on that which we do not understand.
We have faith.
We have courage.

Keep us from all fear today.
Open our hearts to the gifts of this moment,
and bind us to the great unknown with
complete trust.

Assist us in forming a loving image of the
ultimate mystery,
to have faith, and
the courage to give ourselves hope.

An Evening Prayer

Incomprehensible, unrevealed,
spirit of all that exists,
the means of all relationships —
we confess that we have closed ourselves off
from the full joy of existence.

We confess that we have failed to
open ourselves
to a relationship of radical and complete trust
with every person and experience of this life.

We confess that we have failed
to love our experience of the Infinite
in this life
by loving our neighbors as ourselves,
and thus,
in thought, word, and deed we have lost the
way to the only true security and peace.

Therefore we renew our effort to have
a sympathetic relationship with every person,

to live in faith that an unfathomable,
magnificent nature
expresses itself in every moment
and in every experience
of our fleeting passage here.

We confess that we have been afraid,
we have been restless,
we have been unhappy,
we have been wanderers,
lost in a garden we could not see.

We regret our weaknesses,
and we seek a new beginning,
so that we may truly live this life
in the full promise of our time.

We know that there is an enormous power
inherent in each of us, at every moment
in time,
to experience the unbounded love
and deep joy
of the kingdom of God within us.

We remind ourselves that our experience of
the infinite,
the hidden and hallowed power,
comes through our experience of this
creation,

and in our relationship with one another,
and that we have been granted the faculty
to change our universe
by changing our relationship with it.

This is the great gift we have been granted —
the potential to experience all that comes to
us in this life
in complete confidence, love, and joy;
to have the courage and strength
to put aside fear and despair,
and to live each day
in unquestioning trust
in the divine providence
which has brought us into being.

We humbly acknowledge
that despite the magnitude of our faults,
and the number of our failings,
the inexplicable drive of creation,
the sacred spirit manifest in all that is,
continuously sustains us,
and allows us to begin again at any time,
infused with the might
from which we can never be separated.

An Example of a
Weekday Schedule with
Seven Stopping Points

Throughout each day we must continually ingrain in ourselves the habit of being compassionate. Our goal should be to stop several times each day, to remind ourselves to be instruments of loving kindness. Consider how impossible it would be to do this every day for a lifetime and be miserable. Each day we must repel apprehension, melancholy, and selfishness. By repetition of our meditations, and training ourselves daily to express love and joy and thanksgiving, we will come to have the peace and stability that we seek.

This outline, of course, will suit hardly anyone. It is intended as a starting point for a personal design. We must exercise discipline in order to take control of our time; it is our ultimate currency. We must be careful how we spend it; we should fill it with humility, love, and compassion.

6:45 A.M.—7:15 A.M.
Reading and Meditation
Meditate in the same place each day.
Be thankful.

Breakfast
Share this time with a family member, if
possible.
If not, read something uplifting.

Commute
Give thanksgiving.
Take this time to center yourself.

Work
Slow down when you feel yourself racing. The
world does not depend upon you.

10:30 A.M.—10:31 A.M.
Say a quiet thanksgiving.
Remind yourself to be compassionate.

Work
If you are tense, stop and breathe deeply.

11:59 A.M.—12:00 P.M.
Say a quiet thanksgiving.
Remind yourself to be compassionate.

Lunch
Eat with friends if possible.
Take time to share.

Work
If you are racing and skimming the surface, slow down.

2:30 P.M.—2:31 P.M.
Say a quiet thanksgiving.
Remind yourself to be compassionate.

Work
You can be efficient without being rushed.
Concentrate. Watch your breathing.

Find satisfaction in doing the work well.

Commute
Say a quiet thanksgiving.
Remind yourself to be compassionate.

5:30 P.M.—6:00 P.M.
Exercise.

Supper
Eat with family, if possible.

Reading, Family
Turn off the television and discover how much more time you have in a single evening. Give

up your evenings to meetings, work, and to the media only sparingly and never without good cause.

10:00 P.M.—10:10 P.M.
Meditation.
Give thanksgiving.
Skip the evening news and discover that the life you are leading is not full of violence and tragedy.

10:10 P.M.—6:40 A.M.
Rest and Sleep.
It is essential to stay well rested.

Lectio Divina
Each day we should expose ourselves to the inspiration of others. Thousands of saints and wise men and women have left us messages of hope and encouragement. Read what is honest. Read the scriptures and the commentaries. Read great literature and poetry. Read the psalms. Read that which expresses the anguish and the exhilaration of experience, and teaches us that we are not alone. Read slowly, with pleasure, and with concentration.

Some Thoughts
for Reflection

For what will it profit them if they gain the whole world and forfeit their lives?

—Mathew 16:25–26

———◆———

The essence of religion consists not in a particular representation of the divine to be grasped statically, but in a dynamic intercourse with the holy. Religion is not a simple act of thinking of or about transcendent objects but a behavior.... Religion is not a theoretical affair, but an eminently practical one... Religion is... worship of Mystery and surrender to the same.

—Friedrich Heiler

———◆———

To speak of God, even for the purpose of denying God's existence, is to "transform" God into the order of creatures, and so is tantamount to destroying God.

—Raimon Panikkar

Indeed, the very claim to "know" God — in any way — is in and of itself idolatry. "If someone, seeing God, knew what he saw, he did not see God," said Dennis the Areopagite, and with him, the greatest part of Christian tradition.

—Raimon Panikkar

You shall not make for yourself an idol,
whether in the form of anything that is in
heaven above,
or on the earth beneath,
or that is in the water under the earth.
You shall not bow down to them or worship
them.
You shall not make wrongful use of the name
of the Lord your God.

—Exodus 20:4–7

It does me good to do difficult things. It does not keep me from having a terrible need of — shall I say religion. Then I go out at night and paint the stars.

—Vincent Van Gogh in a letter
to his brother Theo

◆

The world begins to look more like a great thought than a great machine.

—Sir James Jeans, British Royal Astronomer

◆

Art is the creation of coherent contexts. . . . the mind itself is an art object. It is a Mondrian canvas onto whose homemade grids it fits its own preselected products. . . . The mind is a blue guitar on which we improvise the song of the world.

—Annie Dillard

◆

As life draws near to the end (one never quite believes it) I think rather more than ever that man has respected himself too much and the universe too little. He has thought himself a god and despised "brute matter," instead of thinking his importance to be all a piece with the rest.

—Oliver Wendell Holmes, Jr.

The world is to the meditative man what the mulberry plant is to the silkworm.

—Alexander Smith

For me heaven is an invitation into life, which, when explored deeply enough, when lived fully enough, when engaged significantly enough, is a way of passing into transcendence. In this way finite moments slip into being infinite, timeless moments. I also believe that human life can be lived so deeply, that love can be experienced so powerfully, that incarnation in fact occurs again and again. God is not a heavenly man, an external force, or a judging parent. God is the creating spirit that calls order out of chaos. God is the life force that emerges first into consciousness, then into self-consciousness, and now into self-transcendence, and ultimately into we know not what. God is the love that creates wholeness, the Being at the depths of our being, the Source from which all life comes.

—John Shelby Spong

God is spirit and those who worship him must worship in spirit and in truth.

—John 4:24

The Tao that can be spoken, is not the Eternal Tao. The name that can be named, is not the Eternal name.

—Tao Te Ching, I

The God who lets us live in the world without the working hypothesis of God is the God before whom we stand continually.... the development towards the world's coming of age... which has done away with a false conception of God, opens a way of seeing the God of the Bible... The world that has come of age is more godless, and perhaps for that very reason nearer to God, than the world before its coming of age.

—Deitrich Bonhoeffer

The secret of God in the universe: God is shapeless, colorless, without similarity, whatever form or condition mankind sees or imagines, it is not God.

—Ali Shari'ati

"But" God said, "you cannot see my face, for no one shall see me and live."

—Exodus 33:20